LOST
SHREWSBURY

DAVID TRUMPER

SUTTON PUBLISHING LIMITED

Sutton Publishing Limited
Phoenix Mill · Thrupp · Stroud
Gloucestershire · GL5 2BU

First published 1997

Title page: Maddox store, Pride Hill and High Street, c. 1960.

British Library Cataloguing in Publication Data
A catalogue record for this book is available from the British Library.

ISBN 0-7509-1488-2

Typeset in 10/12 Perpetua.
Typesetting and origination by
Sutton Publishing Limited.
Printed in Great Britain by
Ebenezer Baylis, Worcester.

Dedication:
In memory of two proud Salopians who were always a great inspiration to me:
Dennis Charles Trumper 1921–1991
Geoffrey Archer Parfitt 1926–1996

High Speed Tyres, Hill's Lane, c. 1950. In 1935 Vincent Greenhous formed this new subsidiary company with branches in Shrewsbury and Hereford, and in 1936 in Wrexham. The company specialized in the sale and repair of tyres. A re-treading plant was later installed at Shrewsbury. The premises are now occupied by Lloyds in the town.

CONTENTS

INTRODUCTION

For my third selection of photographs depicting life in Shrewsbury I have chosen views of the town mainly from 1940 to 1965, well within living memory of many people.

Although Shrewsbury and its people suffered hardships and tragedies during the Second World War, the town escaped the hostilities experienced in the larger towns and cities. There were only two air raids, one of which occurred on 31 August 1940 when a single aircraft dropped one incendiary and two high explosive bombs. They destroyed a house on the Ellesmere Road, killing three people.

The first tangible evidence of a conflict was the appearance of civilians carrying gas masks and the increase in the number of men wearing military uniform. Other signs were the number of women taking up the jobs vacated by the men and the arrival of evacuees. The first influx of evacuees was in 1939 but many returned home during the phoney war. A second influx occurred in 1941 at the height of the Blitz, and a third in 1944 when the 'V' bombs began dropping on our cities. Around 500 pupils from Cheltenham College moved to Shrewsbury School and many of the town's schools echoed with unfamiliar accents.

Several large companies moved their employees out to the comparative safety of Shrewsbury. Among these were the Canadian Pacific Railway Co., whose staff lived and worked at the Ridgebourne Hotel, Kennedy Road for five years. The Pearl Assurance took up residence at the Crown Hotel and at Attingham Hall, while a large contingent of civil servants from the Ministry of Supply took over part of the Raven until 1943.

Three factories were also established by the Air Ministry in 1940. No. 3 shop was set up in Vincent Greenhous' works in Old Coleham making tail sections, No. 4 shop at Column Garage made rudders and elevators and at No. 5 shop in part of the Midland Red Garage they made wings for Spitfires. The serious floods of 1941 saw the closure of No. 3 shop which was transferred to Sankey's of Wellington.

Many buildings in the town were commandeered for military use. Troops moved into the Maltings in Ditherington, there was a salvage unit at Monkmoor, the Music Hall was taken over by the Army Pay Corps, while the old Wyle Cop School was used by all the forces as a recruiting office. The Infantry Records Office moved into Whitehall and Mid-West Command set up their headquarters in the Crown Hotel. The public baths were closed in June 1940 to be used for storage and this caused a storm of protest, led by the mayor, who complained that youngsters were going back to the river to learn to swim.

The ARP wardens set up their headquarters at Porch House, Swan Hill. Air raid shelters were provided for all schools and these were available for public use at times when schools were closed. Public shelters were provided in different areas of the town and by May 1940 there was room for 2,569 people. Some of the shelters were situated in cellars of public houses.

Civilians were urged to 'Dig for Victory' and many public places, including the Quarry, were put under the plough. There was a great expansion of allotments and by June 1941 1,300 were being cultivated. The staff of Maddox had a communal garden in Salt's Field near the Kingsland Bridge where employees gave up their evenings and half-days off to grow vegetables.

Maddox store did so much at this time to keep the morale of the town high, by organizing fund-raising events and by the patriotic displays they put up in their shop windows.

With the sudden influx of servicemen several institutions were established to cater for their needs. A Forces Rest Room was provided by the Christian Science Centre War Relief Committee at Talbot Chambers, a Red Shield Club was opened at 32 Castle Street and a British Restaurant in St Michael's Street.

April 1943 saw the provision of an American Red Cross Club in the Raven, which was viewed with awe when compared to our own clubs. In general the American GI settled in well with the locals and several sporting activities took place, which included American football and baseball on the County Ground and at the Gay Meadow. World heavyweight champion, Joe Louis, also visited the town and delighted fans with several exhibition bouts.

From 1939 the RSI was put on a war footing and prepared as a base hospital for war wounded. A military hospital was also opened at Copthorne and both received casualties from Normandy soon after 'D' Day. Radbrook Hall was also commandeered and transformed into a rest home for sick factory workers.

As the war neared an end some regulations were eased. September 1944 saw the end of compulsory Home Guard parades. The units were finally disbanded after a service at St Chad's and a march past through the town in December 1944. Restrictions on blackout were also eased.

The ending of hostilities saw scenes of great rejoicing. Crowds of civilians and servicemen surged through the town. Flags were displayed and the borough police provided music in The Square for dancing. Street parties also took place throughout the town.

As peace-time returned to Shrewsbury full street lighting was restored. Peace also returned to Shelton Road as the nearby Mortar Centre closed down. In February 1946 the first consignment of bananas arrived but individuals were restricted to 1lb per family.

In 1945 there was a pressing need for new houses and pre-fabricated homes were put up by the council throughout the town. The larger, temporary steel houses can still be seen on Crowmere Road and Copthorne. The first brick house to be built after the war was a private home in Greenacre Road, Copthorne. After a slow start due to the lack of building materials, new housing estates started to take shape at Crowmoor, Meole Brace, Springfield and at Meadow Farm, Harlescott where, in November 1952, the mayor opened the 1000th postwar council house and then presented the keys to the tenants Mr and Mrs T.E. Owen. A letter from the then Housing Minister, Mr Harold Macmillan, congratulating the council on their fine achievement was read out by the town's MP Mr John Holt. The building of council houses continued to gather pace and the 2,000th post-war house at 3 Woodcote Way, Judith Butts was ready for occupation by June 1956.

By the mid-1950s the improvement in the standard of living was beginning to increase the demand for private housing. By 1954 what was described by the *Shrewsbury Advertiser* as 'Shrewsbury's most picturesque estate' was well underway at Copthorne Park. In August 1959 a new Fletcher three-bedroomed house at Mount Pleasant could be bought for £1,875 with a minimum deposit of £95. By April 1962 a new site was being developed at Portland Nurseries where a four-bedroomed house with a garage could be purchased for £3,900. It was reported in 1963 that Ashley, Ashley & Newbrook were eager to start building 600 houses on a 60-acre site at Sutton Road, but they had to wait until the following August for planning permission to be granted.

Towards the end of the 1950s the borough council embarked on a slum clearance scheme which broke up many communities. Large areas of Castlefields, Coleham, St Michael's Street and Frankwell were cleared. In October 1959 the residents of St Michael's Street complained that the slum ruins in Derfald Street and Crewe Street were a menace to the safety of their children. A start was made on clearing some of the temporary prefabs in Abbots Gardens and Abbots Road. In New Street Maddox Buildings were demolished and the site now occupied by Frankwell traffic island was levelled.

The economy began to pick up by the middle of the 1950s and the borough and county councils embarked on a number of schemes that were to alter the town considerably. Old buildings within the loop of the river were torn down and replaced with concrete and glass. Throughout the early 1960s a war of words was mounted in the local papers, both for and against change. In June 1960 historian Dr R.E. Rowse condemned the demolition of historic buildings and suggested that the centre of Shrewsbury should be closed to all but essential traffic. In February 1961 a headline in the *Chronicle* lamented that 'so much of Shrewsbury's heritage is being sold'. Two months later another headline read, 'Ancient buildings are holding up town's progress, protest councillors. Down with the old and on with the new.'

By the mid-1960s local attitudes began to change, helped particularly by the formation of the Civic Society in 1963. The group aimed to monitor the welfare and future development of the town. In 1968 the society's reputation was greatly enhanced when it stepped in and saved the Bear Steps complex, which was greatly dilapidated and due for demolition. The restoration won a Civic Trust Award with one of the judges stating, 'With great vision the Shrewsbury Civic Society realized that demolition, which was imminent, would almost certainly have sparked off another wave of destruction of Shrewsbury's remarkably rich mediaeval heritage.'

The Shirehall, Abbey Foregate, c. 1964. Work on the 10-acre site began in July 1963 with Sir Offley Wakeman laying the foundation stone, and was completed by December 1966. The building was designed by Ralph Crowe, the county architect, and was officially opened by the Queen in March 1967. The total cost, including the fittings, was in the region of £2,000,000. The area in the foreground is the new council chamber.

A GLIMPSE OF OLD SHREWSBURY, 1940–1965

The Square, August 1965. The bus station moved from The Square to Barker Street in 1952. For many years the area in front of the Shirehall and the streets around the old Market Hall were used for parking cars. The right-hand side of The Square was closed to traffic in the mid-1980s and the whole area was pedestrianized in the summer of 1996. Unfortunately, the old Shirehall on the left was demolished within a few years of this photograph and the less attractive Princess House erected in its place.

The old Market Hall, *c.* 1942. This building is reputed to have been designed by Walter Hancock, a local man, and built out of Grinshill stone. It was opened in 1596. The figure between the windows of Richard, Duke of York, the father of Edward IV, once stood on the tower of the old Welsh Bridge. The top room acted as a magistrate's court until 1995. The brick structure between the arches is a public air-raid shelter.

The Shirehall extension, *c.* 1965. The new extension to the Shirehall was built in 1933 on the site of Lloyd's Mansion. It was supposed to provide space for offices past the year 2000! The extension stretched to the right, along Princess Street as far as Peacock's Passage. On the corner is a War Memorial. The inscription reads: 'This stone was inscribed in honour of those members of the County Council staff who laid down their lives in the service of their Country 1914–1918, 1939–1945.'

The Square, *c.* 1955. This tranquil view, taken from beneath the old Market Hall, shows why Shrewsbury is called the 'Town of Flowers'. In the background is Owen's Mansion, built for a rich wool merchant in about 1590. On the left is Grocott & Co., a draper's store. Mr Grocott bought the business from Mr Redmayne in about 1900. The business changed hands in 1936 and was amalgamated in 1944 with the Great Northern & Southern Stores. It continued to trade under the name of Grocott & Co. until the store closed in 1963. Copyright © Walter Scott (BRADFORD) Ltd.

High Street, *c.* 1955. It is difficult to imagine today that, until 1933 when the by-pass was opened, High Street was part of the main A5 from London to Holyhead. Ireland's Mansion on the left was built between 1580 and 1590. It was such a large rambling building it was known locally as Ireland's Folly. In 1965 it was decided to replace the timber frontage of Lloyds Bank with a concrete and glass façade. The replacement won a Civic Trust Award in 1968!

Mardol Head/Shoplatch, *c.* 1955. Shoplatch is thought to derive from the place or residence of the Shutte family. The area around the George Hotel, in the centre of the photograph, was once known as Carrier's End. The properties on the left housing William Major's Tailors, the Maypole and Halfords, were sold in 1962 and redeveloped in 1969. On the right we have Jones the Chemist and part of the old Market Hall.

Mardol Head, c. 1965. Mardol Head was known as Lee Stalls until the nineteenth century. The three shops on the right are William Major, a ladies' and gentlemen's outfitter, Kendall's, who sold a variety of rainwear and umbrellas, and Pleasance and Harper, jewellers. Only William Major still trades in the town today. Note the lorry belonging to Boswell's, a company that built many houses in Shrewsbury during the 1960s.

Mardol, VE Day, May 1945. The street was described by the *Chronicle* as having the brightest display. Peace-time lighting was restored to The Square and High Street and both the castle and library were floodlit. Wherever there was light, people gathered. Pride Hill was solid with soldiers and civilians, arms linked, surging up and down singing. In The Square there was dancing of sorts, wherever there was room!

Mardol, *c.* 1955. At this time traffic was one way up the road to Mardol Head. The King's Head on the left was originally known as the Last Inn. It was renamed The King's Head between 1780 and 1820 and the inn is dedicated to Henry VII whose image hangs outside. He entered the town in 1485 in a most unusual way. The story handed down over the years tells how Thomas Mytton, Bailiff of Shrewsbury, swore that the only way Henry Tudor would pass through the town was over his belly, meaning his dead body. After seeing the size of Henry's army, he had a rapid change of heart, but kept his oath by lying down at the gates of Shrewsbury and allowing Henry to step over him. The shop to the right of the inn belonged to the Pickering family, who have since moved across the road. In the foreground is a van of the Lilywhite Laundry fleet based on Whitchurch Road.

Claremont Street, *c*. 1960. This area used to be known as Hound Street or Dog Lane. The new Market Vaults on the right was once called the Golden Hart. It changed its name in 1868 after the Market Hall was built opposite. Next door is Evan's Newsagents now called Claremont News and below that Attfield's, one of the town's largest corn merchants. All the buildings on this side of the street have been replaced, with the exception of the newsagents.

Home Guard stand down parade, Barker Street, 3 December 1944. The streets were lined with people as 600 members of the Home Guard marched through the town after a special service at St Chad's Church. The salute was taken by the Earl of Powis and the men, 'Shrewsbury's Own', were addressed for the last time by their commanding officer Col. F.H. Liddell. As they were dismissed the band played 'There'll Always be an England'.

Frankwell, *c.* 1960. I believe this is the flood of December 1960 when the river rose to a height of 18 ft 5 in above normal. Over 500 homes and business premises were affected in the worst floods since 1947. The new flats on Natty Price's Corner had only been occupied since September but the tenants were saved from the icy waters of the Severn as they had been built several feet above the flood level.

Frankwell, *c*. 1955. A local girl watches carefully as council workers renew the white lines by the traffic signals on the busy Frankwell/New Street junction. The timber-framed cottages were renovated in 1978 and the ground floor changed into shops. Below the cottages we have the premises of Mr Andrews, the local cobbler, and Mr Turner's fish and chip shop. The tall building on the left was erected in 1851 on the site where David Lloyd ap Rogers built a house in 1623.

New Street, *c*. 1965. During the 1960s many areas in the town were decimated by slum clearance and old communities split up as families were moved out to new estates at Meole Brace and Harlescott. These houses are about to be demolished, but the site was left empty for several years until the Frankwell traffic island was opened in 1971.

Gethin's garage, Mardol Quay, *c.* 1946. Edward Francis Gethin, a native of Shrewsbury, was educated at Wrekin College before taking up an engineering apprenticeship in Manchester. He then spent ten years in India before returning to Shrewsbury to open this garage by the Welsh Bridge. A leading figure in the public life of the town for over thirty-five years, he was a town councillor and was elected alderman in 1944. He was also a borough magistrate. His garage closed in 1958, a year before his death, when the council purchased the site for road widening purposes.

Roushill, c. 1960. Roushill was a narrow street leading from Smithfield Road to Pride Hill. The name is probably derived from Rhos, a damp plain or meadow, leading up to a hill. Many of the buildings in this area were connected with the nearby cattle market. Due for demolition in the background is the old market clock. No matter where you were in the town you could always see the time.

The Seventy Steps, c. 1960. This flight of steps gave access between Pride Hill and Raven Meadows. It was one of many of Shrewsbury's famous shuts which are scattered around the town. An earlier name was Burley's Shut, after a painter whose workshop stood at the bottom of the steps in about 1728. It was later known as the Waggon and Horses Shut from an inn that stood at the Pride Hill end until 1883. The shut was re-aligned during the development of the Darwin Centre and now consists of 105 steps.

Pride Hill Chambers from Raven Meadows, *c.* 1960. Until the late 1960s Pride Hill Chambers was divided into a number of offices occupied by solicitors, land agents and insurance companies. Behind the arched wall are the remains of a fourteenth-century house, now McDonald's restaurant. The tower to the left is the garderobe. The large building on the right is the rear of Boot's shop.

Smithfield Road, during a flood, looking towards Roushill, *c.* 1960. Part of the old cattle market wall has been demolished and stands waiting for redevelopment. On the right is the old mortuary, now the Sea Scout HQ. During earlier floods it is reported that 'sportsmen' used to take their dogs down the Seventy Steps Shut to kill rats that congregated there in their hundreds.

Smithfield Road, *c.* 1946. Smithfield Road was constructed between 1832 and 1835, causing the removal of part of Roushill Walls. At that time, it was the first and only road within the loop of the river. The water trough was erected by the Metropolitan Drinking Fountain and Cattle Trough Association of the RSPCA in 1913. It now stands beneath the Frankwell footbridge as a flower container. The toll-house was removed in about 1965 but the houses on the right still exist, the end one now being used as a riverside café.

Chester Street, *c.* 1947. The architecture of Chester Street has changed completely since this photograph was taken. The site on the immediate left is now occupied by Hartwell Nissan, and the Gateway complex was built on the site of Southam's Brewery. The cottages on the right made way for the *Chronicle* car park and, below that, British Rail developed a block of offices. The gallant council worker assisting the lady to dry ground is Mr Evans.

Castle Foregate, *c.* 1947. On the morning of her wedding a young bride finds she has to negotiate the flooded Severn on her way to church. The brick wall on the left is part of the old sorting office. The timber-framed building on the corner of Howard's Bank was demolished in October 1961. J.H. Mitchell used part of the property as a radio and electrical shop.

St Michael's Street, *c.* 1960. St Michael's Street used to start at the Black Horse, the inn at the centre of the photograph. It was first recorded as the Eagle in 1851 but had changed its name by 1856. The garage belonged to George Oakley. On the right is the corner of the old gas works and the junction of Gashouse Lane and New Park Road.

Castle Gates, *c.* 1955. Shrewsbury's historic castle sits imposingly on a hill guarding the only land route into town. It was purchased by the Shropshire Horticultural Society in 1924 and presented to the town. In 1985 it was transformed into a new regimental museum by Mr Geoffrey Archer Parfitt. Under his expert eye the museums of the KSLI, the Royal Horse Artillery and the Shropshire Yeomanry were brought under one roof. He was also instrumental in rebuilding the museum after the horrific fire-bomb attack by the IRA in 1992. Morris's purchased the café from a Mr Davies in 1919. The menu for October 1947 consisted of kidney soup 6*d*, welsh rarebit 1*s* 6*d*, roast beef and Yorkshire pudding 2*s* 3*d*, apple pie or baked marmalade roll 6*d*. A full three-course meal for just 16 new pence.

Meadow Place, *c.* 1950. The street was formerly known as Roushill Walls and is mentioned as early as 1657 when Richard Davies paid rent for a ditch close by. It has also been known as Castle Gates Lane but was given its present name in 1814. A number of the cottages on the left have been demolished to make a car park for the Beaconsfield club on the corner. For many years, local businessman George Oakley traded from premises in this street.

Castle Gates House, *c.* 1940. Was this Shrewsbury's first piece of conservation? The timber-framed house was moved to this location from Dogpole in about 1700 when the 3rd Earl of Bradford built his new town house on the old site. It is reputed that he moved his mistress Ann Smith into the old house. The bay windows were added in about 1912 when the house was restored. The house on the left, known as Castle House, was the home of Dr Aubrey Ireland.

Castle Street, *c.* 1955. This street scene was to change dramatically as the site between the Raven and Marks & Spencers was redeveloped in the early 1960s. The Raven was one of the town's premier hotels. An early twentieth-century guide book refers to it thus: 'The Raven Hotel is essentially homelike and its comfort is undoubtedly increased by many little elegancies that are not usually found in country hotels. The beautiful surroundings are rendered all the more enjoyable by such a resting place, where the cuisine is really good and the tariff reasonable.' In 1955 the premises to the right of the Raven were occupied by Dorothy Perkins, ladieswear, Melias, grocers, and Lennard Ltd, footwear.

Marks & Spencer Ltd, Castle Street, *c.* 1955. The store first opened at 3 and 4 Castle Street in 1909 and was the twenty-sixth branch to be opened in this country. This site just two doors from the original was developed in the 1930s. By the 1950s the company had acquired England's shoe shop and were advertising in October 1961 the opening of their completely modernized store. Today's store was extended to its present size in 1964 when it absorbed the frontage of Frank Newton's, gentlemen's outfitters.

Castle Street, *c.* 1962. Marks & Spencers after modernization in 1961. Shopping then was much more relaxed than it is today, with people parking their vehicles outside the stores they wished to visit. To the left of Marks we have the shops of G. Oliver, who sold shoes, and A.L. Salisbury, who were leather merchants. To the right of Marks is Frank Newton's store. It was known as the 'Big Hat' because of its shop sign, a large top hat the size of two men made out of a piece of zinc sheet left over from the tower of the old Market Hall in Shoplatch. The sign was taken as scrap during the Second World War.

Pride Hill, *c.* 1955. The building on the right was the main store of Morris & Co. Erected in 1927 it was the company's flagship for over half a century. As well as having a huge grocery department, the store housed a fashion salon, café, restaurant and ballroom. The store closed in 1970, but a part of the premises was used by the company until 1973 as a SaveRite supermarket. Next door is another old family business, J.K. Overy, clothiers and outfitters. The business was started in about 1860 by Alfred Overy and the family continued to trade in the town until the 1970s. The building next door was used by Woolworths until 1964 when the premises was sold for £250,000 and became Timothy Whites. Note the policeman of the country force standing by the cross. He is wearing a flat cap. The familiar helmet was not worn in the town until 1957, although it had been worn by the borough force responsible for policing the town before 1947 (see p. 26). Copyright © Walter Scott (BRADFORD) Ltd.

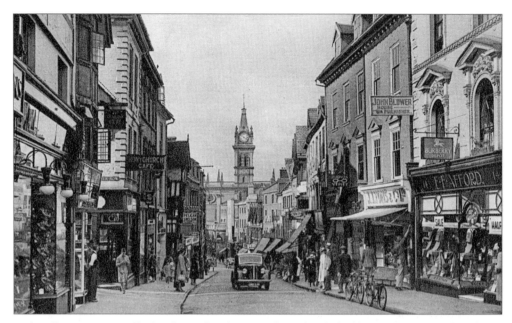

Pride Hill, *c*. 1950. E.F. Afford, tailors and outfitters, are housed in the building on the right. At first glance, the elaborate ornamental frontage looks like stucco but is in fact cast iron from Coalbrookdale. It was made for a Mr Biggs, a florist, and the designs depict his trade. They consist of flowers and fruit, with the head of Pan over each window. Next to Afford's is Lyon's Café and almost opposite a similar establishment run by Mr Honeychurch, two of many such cafés where weary shoppers could take a well-earned rest.

The junction of Pride Hill and High Street, *c*. 1940. PC Dick Chidley was one of the most popular officers on the old borough force. He was promoted to sergeant in the Shropshire force in 1947. He was twice commended for bravery, once for stopping a runaway horse at Mardol Head and again for rescue work after a Mosquito aircraft had crashed on the Berwick Road. He was a keen sportsman and a member of the police concert party where he was well known for his comic routines.

Shrewsbury's General Post Office, *c*. 1958. In 1959 it was announced that the old post office built in 1877 was going to be replaced by a modern building in St Mary's Street. While work was being carried out, a temporary wooden office was erected in St Mary's Place. The new post office, costing around £142,000, was opened by the mayor, Frank Ellis, who bought a 5*s* book of stamps. This corner site is now occupied by Burger King.

Shrewsbury Telephone Exchange, *c*. 1950. The first telephone exchange in Shrewsbury was run by the Western and South Wales Telephone Co. Ltd in Dogpole House from August 1887. In 1914, two years after the GPO had taken control, they moved to rooms over the General Post Office. The exchange expanded in 1926 into the building next door, previously a hotel called the Clarendon.

The Crown Hotel, St Mary's Street, *c*. 1960. This mock-Tudor hotel was opened by the Church Stretton Hotel Company in August 1901. The dragon over the main entrance was carved from oak by a Russian emigré who had fled his country after the revolution. The hotel closed in 1940 and was used as an officers' residential club. It was reopened to the public in March 1948. Unfortunately, the building was removed in 1962 to make way for shops and an office block of concrete and glass.

The Drapers' Almshouses, St Mary's Street, *c.* 1960. The houses were erected by John Carline in 1825 and cost £3,000, which included the land. They were demolished in May 1964. The only part to survive is the coat of arms from over the gateway, which has been incorporated into the new houses in Greyfriar's Road. The old buildings were replaced by the Royal Insurance offices. The architects placed what they described as an 'uncompromisingly contemporary building in the centre of an ancient town'.

GPO Messenger Boys, *c.* 1947. The boys worked from 7 a.m. to 7 p.m. all year round, delivering telegrams on pushbikes in all weather. Back row, left to right: R. Evans (head postman), B. McCreery, M. Rouen, G. Povey, D. Nash, A. Brake, B. Watts, G. Hughes and N. Beaman (head postman). Middle row: H. Russ, A. Corbett, B. Reeves, I. Davis, M. Wallace and F. Birch. Front row: B. Davies, R. Cowley, F. Bradley and D. Eastham.

Fish Street, *c.* 1945. The church of St Julian, or St Julianna as it was first called, is one of the town's oldest churches. The main body of the church dates from 1749 but parts of the tower are much older. The Bear Steps complex on the left occupies the site of the old collegiate buildings belonging to St Alkmund's. The Civic Society undertook the restoration of the buildings in 1968 and now have their offices there.

Wyle Cop, *c.* 1955. Cycling was much safer in the 1950s with fewer motor cars on the road. However, the motor car was beginning to take over and many garages and shops were springing up to cater for them. On the right is Arthur Charles' car accessories shop. He also ran a garage in Frankwell. Just above him is Tanner's wine shop and on the curve of the hill in the timber-framed building is the Nag's Head. Copyright © Walter Scott (BRADFORD) Ltd.

Under the Wyle, *c.* 1945. This photograph was taken from outside the fishmonger's shop belonging to K.E. 'Fishy' Lowe. On the left is the warehouse belonging to R. Maddox who had a large department store in High Street. It was used during the Second World War as a mortuary by the Americans based at Norton aerodrome. Next door is Chong You's Chinese laundry.

Under the Wyle, *c.* 1946. People entering town from Abbey Foregate were faced with crossing two expanses of water. This section was from the English Bridge to the bottom of the Cop. The Midland Red bus negotiates the water quite easily. During the 1941 flood the freezer at the King's Hall was damaged by water. As a result, children in nearby schools got a treat when chocolate bars and tubs of ice-cream, which were thawing rapidly, were distributed amongst them.

Abbey Foregate, December 1960. These were the worst floods to hit Shrewsbury in thirteen years. On the evening of Monday 3 December, shortly before eleven o'clock the river rose to a peak of 18 ft 6 in. Countless numbers of families living in the low-lying districts of the town were forced to move upstairs. Cars were able to pass through Abbey Foregate only if they kept to the centre of the road, which restricted the traffic to moving in one direction at a time.

Abbey Foregate, *c*. 1960. The square-shaped building in the centre was the Bull Inn. One of its best-known landlords was Edward Edwards, known to his friends as Double Ned. He became landlord in 1843. The inn was the venue of a convivial club, supposed to be non-political, but all its members were Tories! The land around the inn was known as the Land of Goshen. Their motto was 'Peace and Plenty'. The inn and the property to the right were removed in 1964 when Lloyds Bank redeveloped the site.

Junction of Wenlock Road and London Road, *c*. 1960. The building on the junction is the Column House, a privately run hotel occupied by Albert Carter in 1964. It was removed when the Column roundabout was constructed and the water trough and milestone were removed to a new site nearby. The old double-decker bus took passengers between the Springfield estate and the town centre.

Lord Hill's Column, Abbey Foregate, *c.* 1950. A great deal of money has just been spent restoring the statue of Lord Hill, causing some controversy. A similar conflict arose in 1945 after one of his arms fell off. After a lot of debate in the *Chronicle*, a poem appeared called 'Lord Hill's Lament'. It ended with the lines:

> Has proud Salopia lost her pride,
> Has she no honour more,
> To leave me to disintegrate,
> And broke for ever more,
> I cannot think so ill of you,
> Salopians, but would fain,
> Believe you'll find a sculptor,
> To make me whole again.

Longden Coleham, December 1960. Planks were laid along the wall of Coleham School and flat-bottomed punts were used to ferry people around the area. One young couple suffered greatly from the flood. They moved into their newly decorated cottage on the Friday only to move out again on the Sunday after receiving a flood warning.

St Julian's Friars, March 1960. We can date this photograph accurately by the billboard on the side of The Friar's fish café. Emile Ford and the Checkmates appeared at the Granada in April 1960. Among his supporting cast were Cherry Wainer with Don Storer and Chick Murray with Maisie. Prices ranged from 4s 6d to 7s 6d. The little hut was a sweet shop run by Mr Dukes who was blind.

Severnside, *c.* 1947. The low land between the old town wall and the river often gets flooded but not usually to the extent of the 1946 and 1947 floods when it was covered by several feet of water. After 1900 the area was developed for recreational activities, such as bowls and tennis. Old Shrewsbury and Severnside both have their clubs based there.

Coton Manor, *c.* 1957. Coton Manor stood, on the site now occupied by flats, on the Berwick Road. It was once the home of John Barker of the firm Jabez Barker. It was sold for him in 1957 by Wiseman & Pook. In August 1962 an advanced residential secretarial training college for young ladies was opened there. The new luxury flats were opened in 1965. A one-roomed flat in 1965 cost five guineas per week.

Monkmoor Hall stood at the top end of Monkmoor Road, beyond the old racecourse, Monkmoor Farm and the old airfield. Built in 1840, it was a large pleasant house with extensive grounds. Early in the twentieth century it was converted into an isolation hospital with fifteen beds. The hall remained the property of the borough council until its demolition in 1961.

LOCAL BUSINESSES

The Little Fruit Market, Bellstone, c. 1960. The Little Fruit Market opened in about 1938 after the street was widened and redeveloped. The shop was owned by S.J. Richards. In 1955 he was also running a similar business on Wyle Cop. The shop closed in the 1960s and is now occupied by one of Sidoli's cafés.

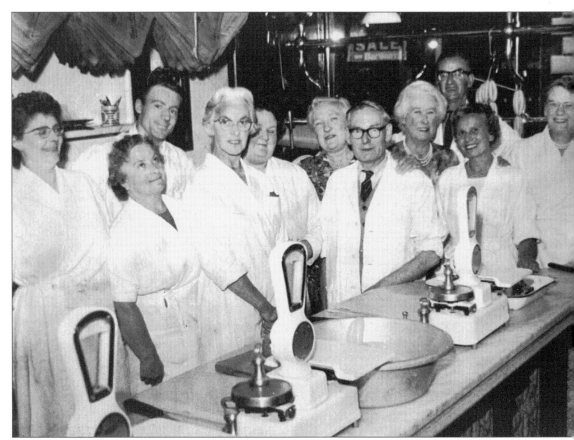

Beddard's bacon curers and pork butchers, Mardol, *c.* 1965. Charlie Beddard came to Shrewsbury in 1913 and opened a shop on Wyle Cop. He transferred to Mardol in 1917. His home-cured bacon and pork pies were renowned for their excellence and the tradition was carried on by his daughters after his death. The business was bought by Gaskell Bros of Warrington in 1965. The staff before the sale, from left to right: Min Morris, Annie Griffith, -?-, Helen Moden, Betty Webb, Mary Beddard, Jack Bankcroft, Edith Beddard, Tom Cowlishaw, Esta Hunter and Mrs Hancock.

Bromley's corn merchant, *c*. 1960. Richard Bromley was born at Yockleton and educated at Allatt's School. In his early years he managed Yockleton Mill before buying it and opening up as a corn merchant in Mardol. By 1905 he had also opened a large warehouse by the Welsh Bridge in Frankwell. Mr Bromley was elected to the borough council for the Welsh ward in 1901 and was mayor in 1925. He continued to trade until the early 1960s. Hall, Wateridge & Owen bought the Frankwell premises, while the Mardol shop was demolished to make a wider access into Roushill.

J.H. Welch, hide & skin merchant, Bridge Street, *c*. 1950. John Welch occupied these premises until around 1964. Not only did he deal in hides and skins, but he also bought old rags. Local children would collect rags and jam jars and take them there just before bonfire night to raise money for fireworks. The gentleman standing by the door is not Mr Welch, as many people thought, but Mr Burke who was the marine or general manager.

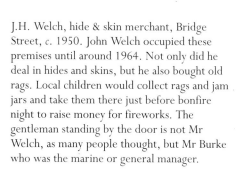

Ankers' fish & chip shop, Claremont Street, *c*. 1960. William Ankers once had two premises in Claremont Street, this shop at no. 5 and dining rooms at 12 and 13 Claremont Street. He took over the business run for many years by a Miss Williams. His brother George had a café at 11 Castle Foregate. Ankers' fish and chips were excellent value and the shops in Claremont Street did a roaring trade, especially on market days and during the flower show.

Ankers' fish & chip shop, *c*. 1960. This photograph, taken inside 5 Claremont Street, shows members of the Anker family and staff. From left to right: Mrs George, Lilly Poole (née Ankers), -?-, John Poole, Lillian Ankers, George Ankers, Mrs Bates and Victor Ankers.

Vincent Greenhous' garage, St Julian's Friars, *c.* 1940. Vincent Greenhous opened up his first business in Meadow Place after moving to the county town from Bishop's Castle. They established links with General Motors and handled such makes as Oldsmobile and Oakland, Marquette, Buick and Chevrolet. When General Motors bought Vauxhall, Greenhous's became one of their first main dealers.

Vincent Greenhous' garage, St Julian's Friars, December 1960. As with most properties in St Julian's Friars, the crash shop was affected by the rising waters of the Severn. The staff on this photograph are back row, left to right: Arthur Phillips, Brian Edwards, Bill Harris, Fred Taylor, Colin Macarthy. Front row: Derek Jones, Jack Davies, Roy Pilsbury. The company moved from these premises in 1995 to a new complex on Old Potts Way.

Medlicott Bros, Frankwell, June 1955. After the First World War John Medlicott served an apprenticeship as a motor mechanic, but soon began to realize the potential of radio and electrical work. He studied the subject and in 1938 founded the firm of Medlicott Bros at the Welsh Bridge. In 1959 they opened new workshops at Green Lane, Meole Brace to complement their headquarters and showrooms at Mardol and their sales and service department at the Welsh Bridge. The business closed in 1994. Notice Bertram Mills' flying elephant in the background.

Sentinel works, *c.* 1944. The rear of the main building which faces Whitchurch Road is on the left and no. 2 shop is on the right. The lorry is bringing in old engines to be stripped down and rebuilt as part of the war effort. The vehicle at the rear is a Sentinel steam waggon.

Gollings outfitters, Grope Lane, *c.* 1938. On the corner of Grope Lane was the Tie Shop established by Thomas Golling. The shop carried a stock of over 20,000 ties, the most representative collection of any private trader in the country, and orders were received from all over the British Isles. Amongst his stock he kept university, old school and all the military colours. The shop was bought by Bradley's of Chester in 1939.

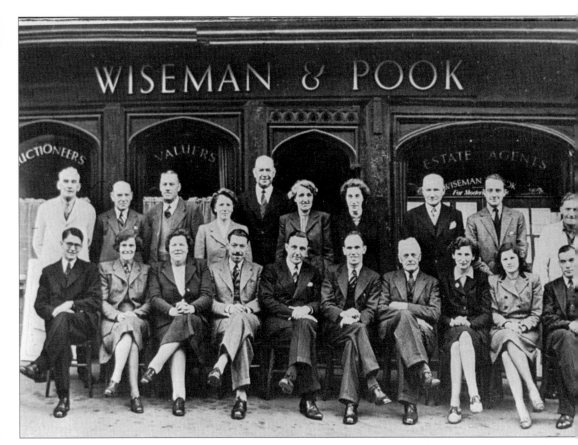

Wiseman & Pook, Butcher Row, 1948. Frederick Wiseman ran his estate agent's business from St Austin's Friars in 1922. The firm was bought by Fred Pook but, although Wiseman played no further part in the firm, his name remained until quite recently. The firm had offices in School Gardens in 1936 and later in Butcher Row, where they also had a sales room. They now have offices on Claremont Hill and in Barker Street after incorporating the firm of Cooper & Green. Back row, left to right: -?-, -?-, ? Hicks, B. Goodbrand, -?-, F. Turner, Alice ?, -?-, John Wilson and -?-. Seated: Russell Wright, -?-, Mrs Burgess, Ralph Ball, Fred Pook, Ron Cotterill, Bob Roberts, Miss Hughes, Miss Peplow and Ken Leader.

Morris's grocery department, Pride Hill, *c.* 1962. Morris's opened Shrewsbury's first self-service shop at their Whitchurch Road branch in October 1949. The venture was a success and more self-service stores were opened at Mytton Oak Road, in 1950, and at Wyle Cop and Woodfield Road in 1951. Pride Hill remained a traditional store until November 1962 when part of the store was made self-service. Photographed in the new section are the manager, Mr Joe Lewis, and Mr Gwilt.

Morris's oil works, Castle Foregate, *c.* 1960. J.K. Morris started to blend oil in 1911 at the rear of his head office in New Street. As trade grew, a new oil works was set up in Rowley's House and the New Ship Inn in Hill's Lane. In 1929 Corbett's Perseverance Ironworks in Castle Foregate was purchased and the oil works were relocated there. A big fire gutted a large section of the works in April 1954, but very little disruption was caused.

Murrells nurseryman & seed merchant, High Street, *c.* 1960. Edwin Murrell traded in Shrewsbury for many years. They had everything for the garden, but roses were always their speciality. As well as the shop they had an extensive nursery in the Column area which they invited clients to inspect, especially in the flowering season of July and August.

Interior of Murrells shop, *c.* 1960. At the flower show in August 1965 Murrells won two gold prizes, one for their exquisite miniature rose garden, which also won gold at the Chelsea Flower Show, and the second for their full-sized rose display which ranged from darkly sensual Lili Marlenes to cold and haughty Icebergs. Mr Murrell is on the right of the photograph.

Adams & Co, ironmongers, High Street, *c.* 1970. The business was founded by R.E. Adams in 1900. In true county town tradition it was an Aladdin's cave, offering customers a full range of ironmongery from nuts and bolts to more sophisticated items of kitchen and bathroom equipment. The two gentlemen are brothers Frank and Harry Wood, the owners, shortly before their retirement. The property was acquired by estate agent John German and converted into offices.

Sheffield's barbers shop, Shoplatch, *c.* 1955. Mr Sheffield opened his barber's shop in the market in 1911 when the cost of a 'short back and sides' was just 4*d*. He was a master barber and continued to practise his trade until the market closed in 1961. During the war he cut the hair of Haile Selassie, the Emperor of Ethiopia, who was living in exile in South Shropshire.

Sidoli's café, The Square, *c*. 1950. Mr Tranquillo Sidoli came to Shrewsbury in 1896 at the age of eleven to work for his brother-in-law in a café in Princess Street. Eventually he bought the shop and established the first of several cafés around the county. On Saturday morning shopping trips you could refresh yourself with a delicious cup of coffee while contemplating which cake to choose from a varied selection brought to your table. Mr Sidoli imported the first expresso coffee machine into the country in 1921 and for two years gave free cups away until the people of Shrewsbury had acquired a taste for it. They also regularly catered for Shrewsbury Flower Show.

Sidoli's ice-cream van, *c*. 1955. This van shaped like a large ice-cream cone was built by Vincent Greenhous. It was a familiar and popular sight around the town during the 1950s. Sidoli's ice-cream is always of the highest quality and they have won several prizes over the years, including the coveted silver challenge cup in 1961, the highest award in Great Britain.

THE MARKET HALL

The Market Tower, c. 1950. The tower of the old Market Hall rose to a height of 151 ft and was surmounted by an ornamental weather vane. The tower was square and had four clock dials illuminated green at night. The clock was supplied by Joyce of Whitchurch and was purchased by public subscription. The following legend was engraved on the regulating dial, 'This clock was erected by public subscription chiefly promoted by H. Keate J.P. chairman of the Markets Committee, H. Fenton, mayor, E. Cresswell Peele, town clerk, Henry Pidgeon, treasurer, Thomas Tisdale, surveyor, Robert Griffith, architect.'

The junction of St John's Hill, Belstone and Shoplatch, *c.* 1960. After road widening in the 1930s, a number of shops were opened under the market, on the Belstone side of the building. Two of the businesses were the Salop Cleaners on the corner and Nicoll's the florist who had traded in Belstone since 1939.

The Market Hall, *c.* 1955. The market was open six days a week, but the principal market days were Wednesday and Saturday. An American visitor wrote, 'We were first struck by the difference in products with those found in the USA. Among the things we at home would not find were rabbits, pigeons, green walnuts for pickling and savoury herbs of all sorts. We also saw home made butter and cheese, poultry products and wonderful fresh garden flowers.'

Mardol Head, September 1961. A firm of demolition workers from the Potteries started work on the Mardol end of the market at 8 o'clock on 26 July 1961. The old clock which had marked the passing of time in Shropshire's county town was stopped once and for all on Saturday 16 September at 4.30 p.m.

Mardol Head, October 1961. Work proceeded rapidly, and by October a great deal of the building had disappeared. The debris was sold from 5s to 15s a ton depending on the quality. Gaffer of the demolition team was Sam White of Newcastle, Staffordshire. He thought that different aspects of the job were dangerous but he felt that this added a bit of spice to the work.

The Market Hall, October 1961. High above the town's streets, Graham Shaw gets to work with his pneumatic drill. Although a great deal of machinery was used, many jobs were done with a pick-axe or sledge-hammer. Average pay was upwards of £12 per week.

The Market Hall, October 1961. This is the view from the tower during demolition. The junction of Mardol and Claremont Streets is on the left. At the top right-hand corner is Timpson's shoe shop. Top left is the furniture shop of E.W. Jones, opened on 24 August 1960 by Lady Isobel Barnett.

The Market Clock, October 1961. In July 1961 the *Chronicle* enquired on its front page if anyone wanted to buy Shrewsbury's biggest clock. There were two bidders. The first was Shrewsbury Corporation, but no one on the council knew where they would put it. The second was Mr Wilmott Wood who wanted to put it over a gatehouse at his headquarters of his poultry business near Craven Arms. One person not sorry to see the clock go was Sidney Bartlett who had been manually winding it since 1934.

The Market Bell, October 1961. St Chad's Church bought the old market bell to be melted down and recast. As the workmen were lowering it down, a coupling broke and it dropped 15 ft and smashed into pieces. The shattered fragments of the bell, worth £200 as scrap, were gathered up and sent to the Loughborough foundry where a smaller bell was cast for the church.

The old and new Market Hall, May 1963. The rebuilding of the market was done in two phases as this photograph clearly shows. Once the Mardol end was ready, in June 1963, the market shopkeepers and tenants moved in on the Saturday and Sunday and demolition workers followed them into the old section of the building. Building of the second half of the new building was expected to take eighteen months.

The junction of Claremont Street and Belstone, April 1963. The shops on this row have only a few weeks left before redevelopment takes place. The butcher's shop belonging to Mr Nutting was previously owned by E. France. In an advert the shop was said to be conveniently situated in the centre of a good shopping area and close to the bus station. Pork sausages were made daily and fresh eggs, poultry and pork were supplied directly to the shop from Mr Nutting's own farm.

The market site, 28 June 1963. The scenes on this page show the accident which happened during the demolition of the old Market Hall. The floor to the cellar collapsed without warning, taking several workmen with it. Stan Hall, reporter on the *Chronicle*, whose office was opposite the site, was first to contact the emergency services who arrived at the scene within minutes. Soon after the collapse, four men were brought out of the debris but it took a further two hours of frantic digging to find the fifth man, who was pronounced dead at the site. The dead man was Kenneth 'Ginger' Cooper from Stoke-on-Trent. As the floor gave way he shouted out a warning to his workmates. But for this, it is believed that other men besides the ones who were injured might have been involved.

The four men injured were Kenneth Davies, who had both feet fractured, Jock Miller, who had a fractured pelvis, Alan Dobson, who had a thigh injury and local man George Arnold. This photograph shows one of the injured being put into an ambulance. Station Officer Jock Buckley was in charge of the rescue operation. Dr Watson, centre left, with his right arm extended, was one of the doctors in attendance. The fireman in the centre with his foot on the beam is Sub-officer Dennis Trumper.

Market site, July 1963. This view taken from Shoplatch covers the empty site to Belstone. One of the biggest snags encountered with the building of the second phase was the foundations for the new tower which had to be dug out by hand by a team of men working shifts around the clock. The finished tower, at 180 ft, is about 21 ft higher than the old clock tower. It is constructed out of 50,000 bricks and crowned by a 40 ft aluminium spire.

The market site to Claremont Street, July 1963. At the same time as the market was being rebuilt, practically the whole of the north-west side of Claremont Street was being redeveloped. The Maypole on the right opened a new self-service store there in November 1961. In June 1964 a restaurant and hairdressing salon were added for the convenience of shoppers.

Shoplatch, October 1964. As the new market hall neared completion a number of road works were carried out. Shoplatch was closed and diversions were necessary. When the scheme was completed the road had been resurfaced and widened to 30 ft.

The Market Tower, March 1965. A giant 100 ton crane with a 240 ft jib was used to hoist coping stones to the top of the tower and to crown it with the gleaming aluminium spire. The *Chronicle* launched a competition to name the new clock and the winning entry was Benbow, a combination of Big Ben and the great Bell of Bow which also referred to the local connection of Admiral Benbow. The topping-out ceremony was carried out on 5 April 1965 by Councillor 'Paddy' Ryan, who climbed to the top of the tower by ladder to lay the last brick. The *Chronicle* warns passers-by to beware, as councillors are well known for dropping bricks.

Claremont Street, 28 September 1964. As cement-mixer driver Percy Lawrence backed his lorry up to deliver some cement to Shrewsbury's new market, the offside of his cab suddenly shot 3 ft into the air and came to rest at an odd angle. He had backed his rear wheel into a hole being dug by the Gas Board. Heavy lifting gear had to be brought in to free the lorry, but Mr Lawrence escaped unhurt. The *Chronicle* remarked that it was very unlikely that his favourite tune would be Bernard Cribbins' 'Hole in the Ground', which was very popular at the time.

FROM THE RIVER

Below the weir, looking towards Underdale Road, 20 August 1965. This is a favourite spot for canoeists and fishermen. Since this photograph was taken, some luxury split-level houses have been built on the bank opposite. The first canoes are just approaching Goff's Island which was created when a barge gutter was cut to bypass a fish weir. The island is now joined by a bridge to St Winifred's. Apparently the Beatles visited the island when they played in the town in the early 1960s before they were famous.

Castle Walk bridge, 1951. The Castle Walk bridge was the first pre-stressed concrete cantilever bridge to be built in the county. It was built in four sections. The central 60 ft span was assembled on the river bank and, once the end spans had been put in place, it was floated down river on a raft and lifted into position by two cranes. The bridge was officially opened in November 1951. It took six months to erect and cost £10,022.

The Severn towpath, c. 1968. From just above the weir to the English Bridge the ground running down to the river is very steep. To stop subsidence this network of concrete terracing was needed below the prison warders' houses. A similar but larger-scale enterprise had been carried out under the old Royal Salop Infirmary in 1959 after a landslide had threatened to drop the hospital into the Severn.

The Council House, *c.* 1960. This view shows the rear of the Council House, a meeting place for the Council of the Welsh Marches. It was formally known as Lord's Place and was leased from Sir Richard Onslow for a term of sixty years. Both Charles I and James II lodged there. William Clement once lived there and until recently it was the residence of the Catholic bishops of Shrewsbury.

Union Wharf, *c.* 1955. The Dominican Friary once occupied this site. In 1823 the land was leased to the Union Wharf Company. The buildings were originally built as warehouses but with the decline of the water trade they were used for a variety of purposes. These included the Lancasterian School, a tavern and as workshops by the antique dealer G.R. Wycherley. In 1973 the buildings were skilfully restored by architects Patrick and Mary De Saulles.

The Basin, *c.* 1955. The Basin is one of the widest points of the river, where the Rea Brook runs into the Severn. A great deal of gravel is washed out of the Rea and has helped to build up the ford on which the English Bridge is built. The houses on the right are part of Carline Fields, demolished in the 1960s.

St Julian's Friars, *c.* 1960. The stone building to the right is a fragment of the refectory, the only surviving part of a friary founded by the Franciscan Order in 1245. The lower section of the buildings to the left, which also contained parts of the friary, were demolished in about 1968. The Greyfriars Bridge was opened on 1 January 1880 on the site of an old ferry owned by William Trouncer, the owner of the old Salop Brewery.

Greyfriars Bridge, June 1961. This mini-armada was mounted by boat users in their campaign to persuade the council to put in a lock or slipway by the weir. The protesters started at the Pengwern Boat Club and sailed down to the weir and back. To date no slipway has been provided.

The Quarry, January 1963. The big freeze started just after new year with a blizzard that left 3,650 miles of Shropshire roads blanketed in snow. Skaters were seen on the river for the first time since 1947. These people are skating opposite the School's boathouse. The police thought that they were taking a great risk; they used loudspeakers to warn them but their appeals fell mainly on deaf ears.

Shrewsbury from Kingsland, *c.* 1960. George Cooper hired out boats from this site for over half a century. The Kingsland Bridge on the right was opened on 28 July 1882. It is known locally as the Penny Bridge after the toll charged to cross it. Top left is the rear of the Eye, Ear and Throat hospital, one of the last surviving pieces of Victorian architecture in the town.

Silk's Meadow to the Welsh Bridge, *c.* 1955. Like the English Bridge, the Welsh Bridge is built on a natural ford. This structure was built in 1795, some yards further downstream than the old bridge. On the right is the headquarters of Morris's, completed in 1924 at a cost of £30,000.

Mardol Quay, January 1959. In the middle of January 1959 temperatures fell rapidly throughout the county and the Severn began to freeze over. This view shows the rear of Gethin's Garage built on the foundations of the old quay. The large manhole in the wall on the far bank, in the centre of the photograph, delivers water from the spring under Princess House in The Square into the river.

Smithfield Road, c. 1955. A young man takes a boat out for a quiet row up the Severn on a beautiful summer's day. The toll house in the centre stood on the site of an old tower in the town's defences. In 1880 the house was lived in by J. Smith, collector of tolls. Before its demolition in 1965 it was known as Corporation House.

Coton Hill, *c.* 1950. The boys are fishing from a punt below the river wall. The cricket ground in Frankwell was once known as Gooseland. The building overhanging the river is the rear of 'Woppy' Phillips's yard. It was taken down when it became unsafe. The building was once part of Barker Bros, timber merchants.

REFRESHMENTS

Princess Street, c. 1950. Shopping was a thirsty business and the Dorothy Café in Princess Street was one of many such establishments where lady shoppers could relax while on an expedition. In 1952 there were more than nineteen cafés in the town centre. Some of the best remembered are Boots, the County Café, the Empire, Honeychurches, the Galleon and, of course, Morris's at the top of Pride Hill.

Barker Street, *c.* 1958. This photograph shows the Little Orchard Restaurant, known affectionately to the locals as the Greasy Spoon. It was frequented by the local teddy boys in the 1950s. The area between Eagle Star House and the Slipper Inn was redeveloped, and Agriculture House was opened there in May 1960.

Church Farm Café, Pride Hill, *c.* 1960. Situated up Owen's Passage between Frank Newton's and Whitfield's was one of Shrewsbury's favourite resting places, Church Farm Café. It was named after Church Farm at Hinstock and in the early years eggs, cream, butter and home-made cakes were brought from the farm for sale at the café. The café contained parts of a medieval hall and Littlewoods, who developed the site, agreed to dismantle it carefully and to re-erect it on another site. Unfortunately, on closer examination it was found that the structure was incomplete and incapable of standing on its own, so it was demolished with the rest of the buildings.

Abbey Foregate, *c.* 1960. The Gay Meadow Café was in part of a house built by a Richard Taylor in about 1842. Mr Taylor was a prosperous maltster and landowner in Abbey Foregate. The café is named after the Gay Meadow, a monastic park belonging to the abbey and extending from the Foregate up to Holywell Street and Whitehall. The origin of the name seems to be lost in history, but it appears to have arisen in Norman times. Shrewsbury Town Football Club's ground is now called the Gay Meadow.

The Elizabethan Room, Morris's, Pride Hill. This café along with the more intimate Tudor room could seat around 300 customers and had the reputation of being the finest in the region. It was very ornate, with fine oak panelling and a plaster ceiling which was a replica of the one in the Bromley Room in South Kensington Museum. This was also the only café in town that the boys of Shrewsbury School were allowed to visit!

Butcher Row, *c.* 1940. This photograph was taken in Butcher Row, looking towards Pride Hill. It shows just how keen the competition for passing trade was at this time. In Butcher Row we have the Greyhound Café, run by Miss S. Clark. To the left on the corner is Honeychurch's Café run by Harold Honeychurch, a fine pastry cook. Directly opposite Butcher Row is Lyon's Café, one of many branches throughout the UK. They came to Shrewsbury in the late 1930s.

The Lion & Pheasant, Wyle Cop, *c.* 1950. This was first recorded after 1780. The last cock-fight to be held in Shrewsbury was held there in May 1857. The house was raided by police and the chief culprits arrested and fined. The inn closed in the late 1950s but re-opened as an hotel and restaurant in 1984 after a great deal of renovation.

The White Hart, Mardol, *c.* 1935. This inn, once known as the Blue Boar, was licensed before 1780. It was owned by F. W. Soames & Co. and had stabling for thirty horses at the rear of the premises into Colehall. The inn closed in 1994. It is recorded that between 1883 and 1958 the town lost over one-third of its public houses. In 1883 there were 153 inns and 24 beer retailers in Shrewsbury. By 1958 it was down to 108 licensed premises. This photograph taken from Roushill shows just how narrow its entrance into Mardol was.

The Victoria, Smithfield Road, *c.* 1960. This inn was set up after the opening of the Smithfield market to cater for the crowds that came to the town on market day. It was first recorded in 1856 and named after the Queen. Earlier this century it was the house from which the Myddle carriers travelled. It had accommodation for twelve travellers in five rooms. There were also good stabling facilities, with twenty-one stalls, seven loose boxes and further loose stabling for another sixteen horses. The inn was demolished in May 1965.

The Horseshoe, Roushill, *c.* 1946. Like the Victoria this public house was set up after the opening of the cattle market, and was closed and demolished in 1965. It was once known as the Three Horseshoes and in the last century had rather a shady reputation, being right in the middle of a red light district.

The Exchange Hotel, Belstone, *c*. 1940. The original building, first licensed in 1868, was demolished in the road-widening scheme of the 1930s, and the new building was built at the rear. Behind the bar is the landlord, Mr John Dixon. In February 1965 it became the first public house in Shropshire to have metered ale.

The Old Crow, Frankwell, *c*. 1960. At one time there were two Crow Inns in Frankwell, this house, which was licensed before 1780, and 100 Frankwell, which is now Everyman's shop. The inn closed in September 1971. To the right is the old Hanwood dairy. The flood is swirling down the aptly named Water Lane.

The Red Barn, Longden Road, *c*. 1950. The Red Barn is first recorded in 1861. Behind the bar is landlord Ron Brookes and his wife Doris. Pulling the pint is his son Colin and on the far left is Mr Samuel Brookes, his grandfather. Amongst the customers are Mr and Mrs Welch, John Cullis, Mrs Phillips, the Woodcock brothers, Michael Clift, George Blent, Joe Williams, Roy Preece and Olive Dixin, the landlady of the Exchange. Climbing up the cage is Polly the Parrot.

STEAM POWER

Shrewsbury engine sheds, c. 1955. The 'Earl of St German' 5050 stands with its back to the round shed.
The fire was taken out by the fire dropper before the engine entered the shed, leaving just enough steam to
berth. On the right is the GWR coal stage. Coal was unloaded from trucks and put into iron boxes on four
wheels, which were tipped into the tenders. Each held 10 cwt of coal and it took ten to twelve boxes to fill a
tender. There was a water tank on top of the coal stage.

Shrewsbury engine sheds, *c.* 1955. The engine is a 'Castle'. The number on the front was a route number which signified a summer train. The building on the left is the LMS coal stage. Unlike the GWR coal stage the coal had to be shovelled up by hand; only later was a crane used. The driver walking away from the GWR shed could be Albert Harris. The ramp on the track worked the vacuum brake. There were two ramps to test the Auto Train Control (ATC) braking system.

Abbey Foregate viaduct, *c.* 1955. This is the Coleham end of the Abbey Foregate viaduct looking towards the sheds. The steam engine is a 'Manor' and the gentleman is H. Gwillam, an old LMS driver. In the centre is the Coleham signal-box, manned in the 1940s by Tommy Hardwick, Albert Townsend and Tom Hyde.

Shrewsbury engine sheds, *c.* 1955. The photographer's back is to Betton Street. These buildings are the old LMS sheds. The chutes on the top of the shed were to allow the smoke from berthed engines to escape. The tall building on the right is the LMS barracks, used as a hostel by rail staff. The steam crane was used for dealing with derailments and at weekends to stack boulders along coastal lines to shore up weaknesses.

GWR drivers, *c.* 1950. Back row, left to right: Joe Powell, Baden Palmer, Bill Barnett, Bill Felton and Evan Roberts. Front row: George Pope, Harry Williams, Frank Padmore and Fred Griffith. These men were all Great Western drivers. They formed a committee to run a social club which organized an annual dinner and evening entertainment for retired ASLEF members. They also organized a Christmas party for the children of ASLEF members. The committee is facing the railway canteen, now the Rea Brook Club. Behind are the old LMS and GWR engine sheds.

The interior of the Severn Bridge junction signal box, *c.* 1960. This signal-box, built in about 1900, is believed to be the largest mechanical box still working in Europe. It is around 70 ft long and contains 180 levers. The box was faced with closure in 1991 but, for the moment, has been reprieved. The signalman is Reg Jones.

Shrewsbury station from the south, *c.* 1955. The large wrought-iron roof was taken down between 1961 and 1962 because of its poor condition. The footbridge connecting all the platforms at this end of the station was also demolished at this time. The cabins on the left were used by examiners, platelayers, LMS guards and carriage-cleaners. The left-hand line goes into the Severn Valley bay. The rodding between the lines is from the Severn Bridge signal-box.

Castle Foregate, March 1962. Railway engineers worked round the clock to replace one of the two bridges which takes trains over the Foregate. The one being replaced was the cast-iron arched bridge which was over a century old. It was replaced by a straight girder bridge designed at Paddington. The work was scheduled to last four weeks and for much of that time road traffic was diverted through Cross Street while rail traffic was re-timed over the other bridge.

LEISURE TIME

The English Bridge on a quiet, sunny summer's afternoon. The girls in their bathing costumes are perhaps going for a paddle from the beach below the bridge. Someone has left a bicycle unlocked and unattended knowing that it will still be there upon return.

VE party, Hafren Close, May 1945. To celebrate the end of the war in Europe parties were organized all over the town. This gathering shows children from the Hafren Road and Copthorne areas. The young boy second from the left is Keith Baxter and next to him is Keith Willocks. Some of the children were evacuees from Liverpool.

Court 10, Frankwell, VJ party, August 1945. Once again the people of Shrewsbury managed to conjure up more food from their meagre supplies to celebrate the end of hostilities. Court 10 was known as Bakehouse Passage and most of the people celebrating are members of the Rhodes and Walker families. The lady wearing the American army hat later sailed out to the USA to be reunited with her GI husband.

Pat Collins' fair, Frankwell, *c*. 1960. Fun-fairs and circuses were always held in Frankwell on a site now occupied by the car park. The fair would visit the town twice a year and locals believed that its arrival always heralded a period of rain! The dive bomber in the foreground was a great favourite, along with the big wheel, over the sticks and the waltzers. In the late 1950s each ride cost 6*d*.

Bridge Street/Mardol Quay, May 1961. Bertram Mills' circus visited the town between 1 and 6 May 1961. Leading the procession from the railway station to Frankwell was this elephant driving his own car. The big top was centrally heated for the two daily performances and prices ranged from 5*s* to 12*s* 6*d*. Other circuses visiting Shrewsbury at this period were Billy Smart's and Chipperfield's.

The John Whalley Organization, Morris's Café, Pride Hill. This was the second annual combined staff dinner, held on 3 December 1948. The firms belonging to the organization were Castle Foregate Motor Co., James' Garage Ltd, Dorrington Garage, Furrows Ltd and Deemster Investment Trust Ltd. During the evening John Whalley presented engraved solid gold watches to Ted Foulkes of Furrows and Charlie Downes, Bill Harris and Dick Milligan of James' Garage for twenty-five years' loyal service. After the dinner and the toasts a number of variety acts were performed by Bert Hollman Productions.

Lewis' Ballroom, Castlefields, *c.* 1950. The New Hall in New Park Road was known locally as Lewis' Ballroom. It was a very popular rendezvous throughout the 1930s and 1940s. The proprietor was Gresley Lewis who was also a local baker. During the 1960s the Studley Club took over the premises.

St George's Infants School, December 1953. One of the highlights of the school year was the Christmas party. Under the supervision of teachers, Mrs Edwards and Miss Bray, the schoolroom is transformed. The two boys at the front are cousins, Alan and Paul Thomas. At the head of their table are Vicky Mastyn and Philip Doster. Second from the right at the back is Paul Deegan.

Shrewsbury fire station, 1 January 1953. A Christmas party was held for the children of Shrewsbury firemen and for twenty orphans from Besford House. After the tea the children were entertained by Hal Monty who was appearing at the Granada in the pantomime *Babes in the Wood*. He was a comedian and conjurer and he entertained the children by making animals out of balloons. The pianist is Ron Ireland, a local printer. In the top right hand corner are Arthur and Eileen Corfield. The boy kneeling with the glasses is Stuart Foley.

Frankwell Carnival, August 1954. The carnival was opened by the deputy mayor of Shrewsbury, Alderman James MacNamara, who owned a butcher's shop in New Street. His wife is sitting to the right of him. The carnival queen was Edith Cadman of Harlescott and sitting next to her is the runner-up, Myra Bennett of Frankwell. Sitting on the far left is Tom Cartwright, chairman of the carnival committee and a local newsagent and grocer.

Frankwell Carnival, August 1954. The carnival parade started and finished on Frankwell's County Ground, where an afternoon of entertainment was organized. One of the highlights which kept crowds thoroughly entertained was the greasy pole. Try as they might no one managed to reach the top and collect the 10s prize. The Hawaiian 'lady' keeping an eye on the proceedings is Wallace Steventon. The young boy kneeling to the right of the pole is Malcolm Newton.

Frankwell Carnival, New Street, *c*. 1947. This entry, known as Combined Operations as all the members were wearing military uniform, was photographed outside Mrs Gibbons' shop. Left to right: Luke Welsby, Hubert Morley, Phil Rogers and Len Bennett. The pony and trap belonged to Mr Welsby.

Frankwell Carnival, September 1953. In September 1953 Queen Salote of Tonga, who had made such an impact at the coronation, paid a surprise visit to the Little Boro'. From left to right: Lord Chamberlain (T. Cartwright), Queen Salote (A. Wagstaffe), Tongan beauties (B. Chant, J. Foley, W. Lock, C. Bebbington and P. Millington). Guards at the front are Buster Jones and Jack Thorpe.

Shrewsbury Athletics Club, 1963. The club was founded in September 1958. Its co-founders were Roger Davies and Alderman Tudor Owen. The club's first president was Alderman Sam Powell, licensee of the Old Post Office and a man who had been greatly involved with sport all his life. In 1961 the club gained promotion to division two of the Birmingham and District cross-country league and was unbeaten throughout the season over its own course. During the 1962 summer season the club was beaten only once, by Birchfield Harriers. Their victories included a win over Guinness Athletics team at Park Royal, London and over Wolverhampton and Bilston, one of the Midlands' strongest sides. The club trained at the Technical College track during the summer and at Shrewsbury School's gymnasium during the winter. Back row, left to right: David Lea, Peter Fairbrother, David Thomas, John Bevan, Julian Lewis, Ben Norton, Ian Leath, David Trumper, Evan Williams and Keith Willocks. Front row: David Edge, Peter Vagg, Nigel Roberts-Powis, David Cookson, Derek Tart, Ken Evans, ? Page, David Evans and ? Page.

Shropshire police force, 'G' division, *c.* 1950. 'G' Division of the County police force were the Shrewsbury policemen. They played games on a friendly basis against the fire brigade, the ambulance service and other local sides. The team was photographed on Frankwell's County Ground. Back row, left to right: Bob Hindmarsh (coach), Bob Taylor, Bill Hunt, Bernard Davies, Neville Roberts (goalkeeper), Bill Jackson, Jeff Tricker, Jack Leighton (trainer) and referee unknown. Front row: Fred Sandland, Jock Barclay, Bob Landers (captain), Pete Evason and Dickie Blyth.

The Quarry playground, *c.* 1955. Immediately after the war a great many schemes were discussed concerning improvements to the Quarry. One of the plans implemented was the opening of a children's playground in September 1946. A great deal of controversy surrounded the playground when the borough council refused to let it open on Sundays. What was known as the 'battle of the playground' raged for several months and a petition of over 2,000 signatures was sent to the council, who were forced to back down early in 1947.

Shrewsbury Baths, *c.* 1955. The baths were opened in 1894 and were replaced in about 1966. For many years the Derbyshire family were superintendents at the baths and taught generations of children to swim. The fancy dome roof covered the administration area, while the glass roof to the left covered the long plunge, where swimming galas were held. Both the long and short plunges have been incorporated into the new complex.

Guide and brownie parade, The Quarry, 18 June 1953. A coronation commemoration service was held in St Chad's church for over 2,000 brownies, guides, rangers, cadets and guiders from all over Shropshire. The event was also attended by Lord Bridgman, Lord Lieutenant of Shropshire, Lord Powis, scout commissioner, Mr Denis Salt, representing Shrewsbury scouts, Councillor Arthur Jones, representing the mayor, Archdeacon Beavan of Ludlow and Mrs Cock, founder of the guides in Shropshire. After the service the guides and brownies assembled in the Quarry where hundreds of spectators had gathered to watch the Lord Lieutenant take the salute. The brownies went in ranks of sixes, wearing gold-coloured reins for their 'run past'. Then the guides, headed by the St John's Ambulance band, marched smartly past the saluting base.

DOWN WITH THE OLD,
UP WITH THE NEW

Frankwell, c. 1964. In March 1960 the council decided to demolish all the houses bounded by Frankwell, Chapel Street and New Street. After some delay this was done, with the exception of the old Co-op which was left standing for several years while its fate was decided. It had been hoped that the council would purchase it for about £6,000 and use it as a folk museum. Eventually the building was sold to Avonscroft Museum where it is now the ticket office and shop. During this time, the open area, which is now Frankwell traffic island, provided free parking for visitors to the town.

Barclay's Bank, Pride Hill, May 1958. Barclay's Bank has been in Shrewsbury since 1907. It moved to this site in 1916 after absorbing the United Counties Bank. In 1927 it bought the premises of Morley's Wine Vaults in Castle Street and expanded into them. During the excavations for the new buildings quite a number of medieval items were unearthed.

Barclay's Bank, Pride Hill, June 1959. The new bank opened its doors on Monday 13 July 1959. It hoped to control a large slice of the business from Shropshire and the border counties. The new premises was built with 2-in facing bricks to the frontage with Forest of Dean stone dressing. It also has a Creetown granite plinth and columns at its entrance. The architects were Green, Lloyd & Sons of London and the builders were the local firm of Jenks.

Castle Street, July 1960. It was announced in November 1959 that Woolworths had bought the Raven Hotel and that the restaurant and accommodation would close from 23 November, but that the bars, Saddle Room and garage would remain open for a while longer. In February 1960 a week-long sale of contents was held which saw dealers and the general public rush along to look for bargains and souvenirs. Demolition of the old hotel started in June 1960.

Raven Meadows, c. 1963. This view of the rear of Castle Street from the old cattle market shows that work was well underway on the new premises for Woolworths and Littlewoods and the extension to Marks & Spencers. Marks was the first to re-open in July 1964, followed by Littlewoods a month later. Woolworths opened their new store on 30 October 1964, just in time for the Christmas rush.

The cattle market, Smithfield Road, 31 March 1959. The *Shrewsbury Chronicle* announced the closure of the old cattle market with the headline, 'Going, going gone – old Smithfield comes to an end.' Although inconveniently situated, its departure took away some of the colour and liveliness from the town centre. Its passing was also mourned by many shopkeepers and publicans in the area. The white building in the centre is the Albert Hotel at the bottom of Meadow Place.

Telephone House, May 1962. Plans for the redevelopment of the old cattle market were made public by Laings and the borough council towards the end of 1958. By 1960 a scheme had been drawn up to provide 72 shops, a 400-car multi-storey park, an office block, dance hall and riverside restaurant, bowling alley, ice rink and new hotel. The building of the office block proceeded quickly and the Post Office were able to move in by the end of 1962. The rest of the development did not proceed so easily, and it was not until March 1964 that a modified scheme got underway.

Shoplatch, *c.* 1963. This photograph shows the demolition of another of the town's old hotels. Parts of the George dated back to 1618. Until 1947 Mr Bates Maddison, a former mayor of Shrewsbury, owned the hotel. He also owned the old Theatre Royal which used to be housed in the building on the right. The last owner of the hotel purchased a convertible car with golden door handles which had once belonged to Lady Docker.

Tesco's store, Shoplatch, *c.* 1965. Tesco opened the new supermarket on the site of the old George on 21 September 1965. The ceremony was performed by Miss Silver Gill, nineteen-year-old Debbie Lee who represented Gillette Safety Razors. On the first day there were lots of free opening offers and it was estimated that upwards of 10,000 people visited the store.

The Square, *c.* 1971. This is a view of the buildings on Princess Street across the demolished Shirehall site. The new Shirehall was completed in 1966 and officially opened by the Queen in 1967. Princess House, which was built on this site, has never been popular with the locals and this year, 1997, has needed around one million pounds spending on it. It has also been reported that the new Shirehall needs a great deal of money spent on it for repairs and maintenance.

New Street, October 1959. The buildings that stood on this site were known as Maddox Buildings, named after a local maltster and landowner who lived at Quarry View House. Including the houses that fronted New Street there were fifty-five buildings on this small site. Some of the dwellings near the river were prone to flooding. The new buildings on this site have been set back from the road and they take their name from Mr Maddox's old house Quarry View.

Abbey Foregate, September 1963. Five large houses were removed from this site opening up a view of the cottages on Brook Street. Safeway opened their new store there on 8 August 1964. Their shop contained a bakery, fresh fish counter, delicatessen and a snack bar. They also guaranteed longer shopping hours and cheaper prices. During the first week they offered 5 lb of potatoes for 1s (5 new pence) and minced beef at 3s 6d per lb (17½ new pence). The lovely trees that flanked the Foregate were taken down at this time for road widening.

Longden Coleham, c. 1960. The buildings on the open site were demolished in July 1960. One of the businesses to disappear at this time was a butcher's run by John Evans. The area fronting the river was known as Boathouse Yard. The site was redeveloped and Skinner & Davidson chemist shop opened there. The shops on this photograph were built in the 1930s on the site of Hazeldine's iron foundry.

Bridge Street to Claremont Bank, *c.* 1961. St Chad's School and a number of cottages were demolished to give this open aspect, just before the multi-storey car park was built. The Priory Grammar School was opened in 1911 as a school for boys and girls, though they were strictly segregated. The girls moved to their Longden Road site in 1939.

First multi-storey car park, *c.* 1963. The car park was opened in August 1963 just in time for the Flower Show. As well as a car park Furrows had a filling station and showroom on the ground floor. They also had one of the town's first car washes for just 7s 6d (37½ new pence). It is interesting to note that new parking restrictions and double yellow lines came into the town in October 1963.

Central Avenue, The Quarry, *c.* 1946. The first of the famous lime trees was cut down in April 1945. There was a great outcry, but experts believed that they were dangerous. Many of the trees had large bunches of mistletoe growing on them and others had bees' nests complete with honey. After felling, many were seen to be hollow and they were left to show people how dangerous they were. Planting of the new trees was completed by 1950.

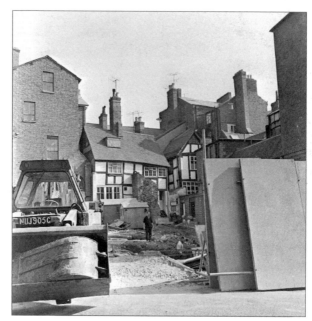

Mardol Head, June 1971. The old buildings at Mardol Head which housed the Maypole, William Major and Pleasance & Harper (see p. 11) were demolished by the firm of J. Parry & Son. The new buildings were ready for occupation the following year. New Day's Super New Furnishing Centre opened there on 14 April. The timber-framed building is the rear of the Plough Inn. After the new buildings were built the passageway leading to the back of the inn was renamed Plough Shut, much to the annoyance of the landlord.

The new telephone exchange, *c*. 1955. By 1950 it became obvious that the telephone exchange at the top of Pride Hill was far too small for modern needs and, with no room to expand, this controversial new site was chosen on Town Walls. Work started in 1954 and the change-over to an automatic exchange took place without any problems on 3 October 1959. The most up-to-date apparatus, known as GRACE – Group Routing And Changing Equipment – was installed in the new building.

Town Walls, March 1957. During the building of the new telephone exchange this bailey bridge was erected at the Beeches Lane end of Town Walls. It spanned a deep chamber which was made in the road to take all the cables into the new building.

Shrewsbury fire station, Cross Hill, *c.* 1955. This station on Cross Hill was built for the old borough fire brigade and was opened by Alderman Ashton, chairman of the Watch Committee, on 30 June 1938. In 1941 the brigade was absorbed into the National Fire Service and in 1948 Shropshire County Council became the fire authority. This station was closed in 1973 and demolished in 1976. This photograph was taken during an HMI inspection. Firemen, left to right: -?-, Dennis Trumper, Jim Jones, Bob Evans, -?-, Jim Prince, -?-, -?-, N. Vanderstay, -?- and Station Officer Jock Buckley.

St Michael's Street, c. 1965. In 1961 it was suggested that a new fire station, incorporating a headquarters for Shropshire and workshops and stores be built along St Michael's Street. From the beginning the idea was severely criticized. By 1965 the council had agreed to develop the site and these buildings known as Shune's Row, which fronted St Michael's Street, were demolished.

St Michael's Street, c. 1973. This view was taken from the same angle as the one above. The buildings on the left are the new workshops and stores. In the centre are the tower and training area which incorporated a smoke chamber, and behind them is an administration block. The men's canteen and living quarters have still to be built.

PEOPLE & EVENTS

St Michael's Street, 6 October 1959. The Bishop of Shrewsbury, the Right Revd R.L. Hodson dedicated new gates to the entrance of St Michael's Church during an evening service conducted by the vicar, Revd G. Owen. The new gates were 4 ft high and made of wrought iron. They replaced high iron gates which had hung off their hinges for years.

Pride Hill, 19 June 1952. During the festivities to celebrate Shrewsbury School's 400th Anniversary this High Cross was presented by the school to the town. The cross was an expression of the school's loyalty to Shrewsbury and the inscription on the monument reads, 'The Royal School of Shrewsbury presents the cross to the town it loves. It changed its site but not its loyalty.'

The Castle, 24 October 1952. Her Majesty the Queen visited Shrewsbury to open a new terrace on Kingsland as part of Shrewsbury School's 400th anniversary. She arrived in the town by train and before making her way to the Schools by car she made a short visit to the castle to meet the borough council. With the Queen and Prince Philip is the mayor, Alderman Col. J.M. West, who was also a master at the Schools.

Police cadets, the Drill Hall, Coleham, 8 October 1964. Sixteen police cadets took part in a parade and inspection. The cadets had just finished a five-week course at Shrewsbury before joining units around the county for the next phase of their training. The inspection was carried out by Brigadier C. Goulburn, who was accompanied by Chief Constable R. G. Fenwick and his assistant chief constable, A. Remie. Back row, left to right: D. Chambers, M. Caddick, W. Hill, J. Culley, T. Dainty, R. Mellor, M. Bowen, H. Greaves, B. Burns. Front row: M. Whitney, B. Kent, P. Roberts, D. Wilde, B. Bill, T. Price, J. Massey.

Labour councillors, c. 1958. Shrewsbury's newly elected Labour councillors had this photograph taken outside the council chamber in the grounds of the castle. Back row, left to right: Wilf Edwards, Ted Hall, George Farr, Mr Burgess, Jim Cox and Vic Pierce. Middle row: Jack Parry, Pete Ellis, Len MacDonald, John Burke, Cliff Smith, Harry Beckett and Sid Osbourne. Front row: Arthur Willis, W.J. Jones, Mrs Lancaster, Alderman Len Tilling (Shrewsbury's first Labour mayor, in 1947), Tom Ryder and Ben Huckfield.

British Legion, Abbey Foregate. The vicar is Father Ralph Lumley who moved to the Abbey Church in 1957. He was appointed rural dean of Shrewsbury in 1962 and three years later he was made a prebendary of Lichfield Cathedral. To the left of the vicar is Mr H. Gee, a local newsagent. He was a life-long member of the Legion and of the Claremont Baptist Church. In the 1959 New Year's Honours List he received an OBE. The churchwardens are left, Fred Pyatt and right, Bill Caswell.

Smithfield Road, December 1960. The local firm of Oakley's came to the rescue when they used one of their tractors to pull this A30 out of the flood. Driving the tractor is Derek Richards with the aid of Norman Clinton. Seated on the bonnet of the car is 'Tacky' Matthews.

Mardol Head to Shoplatch, 24 June 1945. A serious fire broke out at the County Theatre and a large cloud of dense black smoke could be seen drifting over St John's Hill. The whole of the balcony was alight and flames were seen leaping through the roof. The National fire service fought the blaze, playing water down on the fire from a 60 ft fire escape. Cars were removed from the rear of the George Hotel, as was equipment and stock from adjacent shops.

The burnt-out shell of the County Theatre, 24 June 1945. The last film to be shown starred Gary Cooper and Jean Arthur in *Mr Deeds Goes To Town*. The theatre had an unusual rear-screen projection all of which was unharmed. The cinema never re-opened, but was used by Aston's as a furniture store.

Barker Street, 7 August 1966. This devastating fire gutted the premises of A.D. Foulkes and a wool warehouse next door, causing over £1 million worth of damage. At the height of the fire loud thuds were heard as calor gas cylinders and tins of paint exploded in the heat. A much bigger bang was heard as stock and machinery crashed down from the upper floors. A human chain of onlookers was formed to pass boxes of ammunition and explosives from Gordon Forrest's fishing tackle and gun shop which was situated in an arcade threatened by the blaze.

The Shrewsbury to Shawbury road, May 1954. Several passengers were hurt by flying glass when this Midland Red bus mounted the grass verge, struck a telegraph pole and rolled on its side into a ditch. The bus, carrying forty-five passengers to Shawbury, was the 8 a.m. service from Barker Street. The injured were taken to Shawbury RAF hospital but none were detained.

Sundorne Road, 2 July 1955. This photograph shows the funeral cortège of Mr H.F. 'Harry' Turner, one of Shrewsbury's best-known councillors in the 1950s. He was employed by Midland Red and was their resident engineer. A Midland Red coach conveyed the coffin to St Michael's church and afterwards to the cemetery. As the cortège entered the church it passed between two ranks of Midland Red officials and employees.

New Street, 11 April 1963. This accident happened when two soldiers from Park Hall near Oswestry hijacked a Mid-Wales Motorway's bus from Barker Street. Realizing they had driven away with a terrified old lady in the bus, they slowed down over the Welsh Bridge to let her jump off. The bus was then driven at speed up Frankwell and into New Street where they lost control and crashed into some cottages. The area then had to be evacuated because of a strong smell of gas leaking from the cottages. The soldiers were caught and sent to prison for three months.

The Test of Truth, 20 April 1960. Mr Pat Cowhey is seen here taking part in an unusual publicity stunt. Clad only in a loin cloth, he pitted his strength against two horses in the 'Test of Truth', one of the main features of the film *Goliath*, starring muscle-man Steve Reeves, which was showing at the Empire Cinema in Mardol. A former professional boxer, Mr Cowhey had more than 175 bouts between 1929 and 1938, winning over 150 of them. He was also a sparring partner to world champion Freddie Mills. The photograph was taken at a riding school in Racecourse Lane.

The Quarry, 25 June 1964. The Princess Royal was a regular visitor to Shrewsbury. On this occasion she had come to open the Telford Way, a link road first envisaged in the Town Planning Act of 1932, and the new TA centre at Sundorne. She also visited the Quarry to present new colours to the 4th Battalion KSLI. The Chaplain General is Archdeacon I.D. Neil.

Home Guard, officers and NCO's stand-down dinner, December 1944. Back row, left to right: Cpl. Griffiths, L/Cpl. Pugh, L/Cpl. Jones, L/Cpl. George, L/Cpl. Williams, L/Cpl. Evans, Sgt. Newing and Lt. Dyer. Middle row: Lt. Vaughan, Cpl. Peacock, Cpl. Davies, Cpl. Roberts, Cpl. Vickers and Lt. E. Jones. Front row: Lt. Newton, D.J. Edwards (head postmaster), Capt. C. Abraham, Lt.Col. Halliday MBE, Major Bates, Major Morgan, and Capt. Hampton. All the men were from 'D' Company 9th (PO) Battalion, Shropshire.

The Sentinel Home Guard, *c.* 1944. The Shropshire Home Guard was formed in May 1940 and affiliated to the Shropshire Territorial Army Association. From July 1940 they were allowed to wear the badge of the KSLI. At the time of their stand-down in December 1944, over 31,000 men had served in the Shropshire companies. This photograph was taken outside the main entrance to the Sentinel works which is covered by camouflage netting.

St George's Boys School, *c*. 1952. Mr Clarke on the left was the class teacher and also deputy head. The headmaster was Mr Godfrey, right, who was in charge of the school from 1936 until 1953. Among the boys photographed are Stan Humphries, Alan Power, Robert Hands and Keith Willocks.

Longden Coleham, *c*. 1952. The suburbs of the town have always been the strongest supporters of Shrewsbury Carnival. After several loss-making efforts in the early 1950s, the town event folded, but Frankwell held their own carnival until the town felt able to support its own again. Among the characters from Coleham are Eunice and Iris Hall.

Morris's Ballroom, *c.* 1952. This is the staff of Boots shop at their annual dance. The firm came to Shrewsbury in 1902. They have since extended their store on several occasions. Morris's Ballroom had the best sprung floor in Shrewsbury and was used by thousands of local people between 1927 and 1970. It was completely renewed in 1945 after being worn out by the heavy boots of servicemen, dancing the night away!

The West Midland showground, May 1955. The show held in 1955 was described as a mudbath. One veteran claimed he had not seen anything like it since Flanders in 1917. An exhibitor's stand selling gum boots cleared its stock in record time and had to send out for more. By 1956 1¼ miles of permanent roads had been laid around the ground to prevent a recurrence of the situation.

A meeting of Shrewsbury JPs, *c.* 1965. Shrewsbury magistrates held their annual dinner on this occasion at the Radbrook Hall Hotel. Back row, left to right: Jack Smout, Frank Leath, Kenneth Bevan, Stanley Booth, A.T. Davies, Col. Careless, Bernard Lingen, Wilf Edwards and John Wall. Middle row: Mary Taylor, Jane Kelly, George Dodd, Douglas Draycott (recorder) and Tom Bowdler. Front row: Audrey Kempster (daughter of Mrs Marion Wallace Cock), Lena Phillips, Florence Puddle, Alderman Mrs Lancaster and Freda Pierce.

Salop Licensed Victuallers' Ladies Auxiliary Association, 13 November 1956. This was the seventh annual banquet and it was held at the Raven Hotel. The group was formed in 1950 and was very successful in raising money for local charities. The menu consisted of paté de Strasbourg or cream of asparagus soup, Norfolk duckling, stuffing and apple sauce, minted garden peas, roast potatoes and peach melba or cheese and biscuits followed by coffee. Back row, left to right: Mrs Grierson, Mrs Walters, Mrs Renshaw, Mrs Clift, Mr Murphy, Mrs Green, Mrs Cock (Mayor), Mr Honey (banquet chairman), Mrs Pryce, Mrs Middleton (treasurer), Mrs Joyner, Mrs Russell, Mrs Earl and Mrs Humphreys. Front row: Mrs Davies, Mrs Lingen, Mrs Murphy, Mrs Kemmy (secretary), Mrs Dixon (president), Mrs Reade (vice-president), Mrs Manning and Mrs Kay.

The Swan, Frankwell, *c*. 1960. Bert Chant was the first person to receive the Wallace Steventon Memorial salver for dominoes. Left to right: Geoff Bebbington, Bert Chant, Jack Clift, Mrs Steventon, Gordon Galliers and Arthur Mansell. Mr Steventon, known locally as 'Gudgeon', was a well-known character in the Little Boro'.

The Abbey parish hall, *c*. 1958. Every year in October the parish held a sale of work and all the money raised was sent to USPG to help with worldwide missionary work. The three lady helpers from the right are: Mrs Morris, Mrs Caswell and Mrs Medlicott.

Shrewsbury Carnival, the Quarry, 1952. J. Hughes gained first prize for his portrayal of Mexican revolutionary leader, Zapata. He was also advertising the film *Viva Zapata* which was being shown at the Empire cinema. In the film the part of Zapata was played by Marlon Brando. Anthony Quinn won the Oscar for best supporting actor for playing Zapata's loutish brother.

ACKNOWLEDGEMENTS

Once again I am grateful to so many people for their kindness and generosity in trusting me with their photographic treasures. In particular I would like to thank those listed below for items used in this book: Abbeycolor, Mr D. Benson, Mrs D. Caswell, Mr M. Causer, Mr P. Cowhey, Mr and Mrs Cowlishaw, Mr F. Davies, Mr Len Davies BEM, Mr and Mrs I. Davies, Mr K. Easom, Mrs J. Edwards, Mrs G. Fallows, R. & J. Gamble, Greenhous Shrewsbury Ltd, Mr R. Griffith, Mrs Hepworth, Mrs Hughes, Mr P. Hughes, Mr R. Hughes, Mr J. Kelsall, Local Studies Library, Mr J. Mabbott, Mr R. Mellor, Mr R. Mulford, Mrs H. Moden, Morris & Co., Miss M. Murray, Mr R. Pilsbury, Mr J. Pook, Mr J. Powell, F. & B. Preen, Mrs Price, Mr A. Roberts, Mr N. Roberts, Walter Scott Collection, Mrs Sevington, Mrs E. Tench, Mr G. Thomas, Mrs M. Thomas, Mr Tipton, Mr H. Turner, Mr N. Turner, Mr Wood, Mr D. Woodhouse.

I would also like to thank Tony Carr and all the staff at Shrewsbury Records and Research Centre for their patience and help. I am also grateful to Ron Bedford, Mr L. Bennett, Mr H. Corfield, Mr L. Davies BEM, Mr F. Leath OBE, Mr A. Love, Mr J. Powell and Mr H. Turner for sharing their memories with me. I am indebted to the *Shrewsbury Chronicle and Advertiser*, in particular for the editions covering the 1940s, '50s and '60s, from which I have gleaned so much knowledge and information. I am greatly indebted to Mr Robert Evans of Abbeycolor for his help and advice in preparing the photographs for this publication and to my wife Wendy for her assistance and work at the keyboard.

BRITAIN IN OLD PHOTOGRAPHS

Lincoln
Lincoln Cathedral
The Lincolnshire Coast
Liverpool
Around Llandudno
Around Lochaber
Theatrical London
Around Louth
The Lower Fal Estuary
Lowestoft
Luton
Lympne Airfield
Lytham St Annes
Maidenhead
Around Maidenhead
Around Malvern
Manchester
Manchester Road & Rail
Mansfield
Marlborough: A Second Selection
Marylebone & Paddington
Around Matlock
Melton Mowbray
Around Melksham
The Mendips
Merton & Morden
Middlesbrough
Midsomer Norton & Radstock
Around Mildenhall
Milton Keynes
Minehead
Monmouth & the River Wye
The Nadder Valley
Newark
Around Newark
Newbury
Newport, Isle of Wight
The Norfolk Broads
Norfolk at War
North Fylde
North Lambeth
North Walsham & District
Northallerton
Northampton
Around Norwich
Nottingham 1944–74
The Changing Face of Nottingham
Victorian Nottingham
Nottingham Yesterday & Today
Nuneaton
Around Oakham
Ormskirk & District
Otley & District
Oxford: The University
Oxford Yesterday & Today
Oxfordshire Railways: A Second
   Selection
Oxfordshire at School
Around Padstow
Pattingham & Wombourne

Penwith
Penzance & Newlyn
Around Pershore
Around Plymouth
Poole
Portsmouth
Poulton-le-Fylde
Preston
Prestwich
Pudsey
Radcliffe
RAF Chivenor
RAF Cosford
RAF Hawkinge
RAF Manston
RAF Manston: A Second Selection
RAF St Mawgan
RAF Tangmere
Ramsgate & Thanet Life
Reading
Reading: A Second Selection
Redditch & the Needle District
Redditch: A Second Selection
Richmond, Surrey
Rickmansworth
Around Ripley
The River Soar
Romney Marsh
Romney Marsh: A Second
   Selection
Rossendale
Around Rotherham
Rugby
Around Rugeley
Ruislip
Around Ryde
St Albans
St Andrews
Salford
Salisbury
Salisbury: A Second Selection
Salisbury: A Third Selection
Around Salisbury
Sandhurst & Crowthorne
Sandown & Shanklin
Sandwich
Scarborough
Scunthorpe
Seaton, Lyme Regis & Axminster
Around Seaton & Sidmouth
Sedgley & District
The Severn Vale
Sherwood Forest
Shrewsbury
Shrewsbury: A Second Selection
Shropshire Railways
Skegness
Around Skegness
Skipton & the Dales
Around Slough

Smethwick
Somerton & Langport
Southampton
Southend-on-Sea
Southport
Southwark
Southwell
Southwold to Aldeburgh
Stafford
Around Stafford
Staffordshire Railways
Around Staveley
Stepney
Stevenage
The History of Stilton Cheese
Stoke-on-Trent
Stoke Newington
Stonehouse to Painswick
Around Stony Stratford
Around Stony Stratford: A Second
   Selection
Stowmarket
Streatham
Stroud & the Five Valleys
Stroud & the Five Valleys: A
   Second Selection
Stroud's Golden Valley
The Stroudwater and Thames &
   Severn Canals
The Stroudwater and Thames &
   Severn Canals: A Second
   Selection
Suffolk at Work
Suffolk at Work: A Second
   Selection
The Heart of Suffolk
Sunderland
Sutton
Swansea
Swindon: A Third Selection
Swindon: A Fifth Selection
Around Tamworth
Taunton
Around Taunton
Teesdale
Teesdale: A Second Selection
Tenbury Wells
Around Tettenhall & Codshall
Tewkesbury & the Vale of
   Gloucester
Thame to Watlington
Around Thatcham
Around Thirsk
Thornbury to Berkeley
Tipton
Around Tonbridge
Trowbridge
Around Truro
TT Races
Tunbridge Wells

Tunbridge Wells: A Second
   Selection
Twickenham
Uley, Dursley & Cam
The Upper Fal
The Upper Tywi Valley
Uxbridge, Hillingdon & Cowley
The Vale of Belvoir
The Vale of Conway
Ventnor
Wakefield
Wallingford
Walsall
Waltham Abbey
Wandsworth at War
Wantage, Faringdon & the Vale
   Villages
Around Warwick
Weardale
Weardale: A Second Selection
Wednesbury
Wells
Welshpool
West Bromwich
West Wight
Weston-super-Mare
Around Weston-super-Mare
Weymouth & Portland
Around Wheatley
Around Whetstone
Whitchurch to Market Drayton
Around Whitstable
Wigton & the Solway Plain
Willesden
Around Wilton
Wimbledon
Around Windsor
Wingham, Addisham &
   Littlebourne
Wisbech
Witham & District
Witney
Around Witney
The Witney District
Wokingham
Around Woodbridge
Around Woodstock
Woolwich
Woolwich Royal Arsenal
Around Wootton Bassett,
   Cricklade & Purton
Worcester
Worcester in a Day
Around Worcester
Worcestershire at Work
Around Worthing
Wotton-under-Edge to Chipping
   Sodbury
Wymondham & Attleborough
The Yorkshire Wolds